# Spiritual Guidance *for* Common People

Carolyn Simmons

Uriel Press

Copyright © 2023 Carolyn Simmons.

All rights reserved. No part of this book may be used or reproduced by any means, graphic, electronic, or mechanical, including photocopying, recording, taping or by any information storage retrieval system without the written permission of the author except in the case of brief quotations embodied in critical articles and reviews.

Uriel Press books may be ordered through booksellers or by contacting:

Uriel Press
1663 Liberty Drive
Bloomington, IN 47403
www.urielpress.com
844-752-3114

Because of the dynamic nature of the Internet, any web addresses or links contained in this book may have changed since publication and may no longer be valid. The views expressed in this work are solely those of the author and do not necessarily reflect the views of the publisher, and the publisher hereby disclaims any responsibility for them.

Any people depicted in stock imagery provided by Getty Images are models, and such images are being used for illustrative purposes only.
Certain stock imagery © Getty Images.

Scripture quotations are taken from the Holy Bible, New International Version®, NIV®. Copyright © 1973, 1978, 1984 by Biblica, Inc.™ Used by permission of Zondervan. All rights reserved worldwide.

ISBN: 979-8-8861-2021-9 (sc)
ISBN: 979-8-8861-2022-6 (e)

Library of Congress Control Number: 2023917653

Print information available on the last page.

Urial Press rev. date: 10/26/2023

This book is dedicated to my mother, Ethel Robinson who has taught me more than any life experience could ever teach me. Thank you, mom!

# Be Kind

Has anyone told you, be kind? It is so easy to be kind when others are kind to you. But what happens when you don't receive kindness in return? For most people retaliation and a vicious word, or a snippety remark will be your reaction. We must understand our boundaries and our limits. When you feel your kindness is taken as a joke kindly remove yourself from the situation. We can see many examples where Biblical Personalities were treated not so kindly. The Leper in the Bible was scorned for the disease that afflicted him daily. It was a loathsome disease. You stayed outside the city or village in a Leper's Camp. A man full of leprosy came and knelt before Him and inquired of him saying, "Lord, if you are willing, you can make me clean? (Matthew 8:2). Jesus was kind and had compassion. He had a kind heart. Kindness is difficult when your heart is not so kind. The Bible also says, "Kind words turn away wrath." (Proverbs 15:1).

# The Heart

There once lived a wealthy Madam. Her inner circle consisted of people like her, movers and shakers, the pillars of the community. She dressed well, lived well, and had the finest of China. Her travels were second to none. She gave to the underprivileged only when recognition was given. This woman had a housekeeper that was very modest. She did not have much, but she shared all she had. One day Madam had a party and afterwards she had much food leftover. She instructed the housekeeper to bag up as much as she could and give to her wealthy guest. As the guest exited the party some of them disposed of the food and others gave it away. Not one time did Madam offer the housekeeper any food. A few days later Madam fell extremely ill. Her heart was failing and she needed a heart transplant. All the money in the world could not acquire a compatible heart. As her health declined the housekeeper began to stay by her side morning, noon, and night. One cold and frigid morning the housekeeper started out to the market. On the way to the market the housekeeper was tragically hit by a car and killed. The days that followed Madam underwent heart surgery. As Madam gained strength, she had flowers sent to the housekeeper's family, cheap, nonetheless. She also inquired as to who donated her heart. The doctors told her the heart was the healthiest heart they have ever seen. Madam thought to herself that it must be a wealthy person that donated the heart, because only wealthy people can have a heart like that. She instructed her banker to draw-up a sizable check. The banker investigated as to whom the check was to be given. He saw it was to be given to the housekeeper's family. Madam was astonished. She contacted the family of the housekeeper and asked, why her? The family read a handwritten will off a brown paper bag: To Madam who is ill, may God bless you with a healthy heart. I am so ever grateful to you. You have employed me for 25 years, which helps me to provide for my family. So, if anything should happen to me before you receive your heart, I give you, my heart.

Hezekiah Walker's gospel song sums it all up, because "I'm grateful, grateful, so grateful just to praise you Lord." flowing from my heart are the issues of my heart, is gratefulness.

What is flowing from your heart?

# Temptation

When evil is all around you what do you do? Temptation increases when evil rears his head up. You have to be mindful not allowing your desires to tempt you. Sometimes you feel you are the underdog, and the doormat, to the evil that lurks around you. But God wants you to stand up against the wiles of evil. Put on the full armor of God, so that you can take your stand against the devil's schemes, Ephesians: 6-11. The scripture goes on to say We do not fight against flesh and blood. So if it is not human it must be a supernatural evil. Evil is all around us. Do not repay evil or insult. On the contrary, repay evil with blessing, kind loving disposition. God wants you to know the world has nothing to offer. Hold on and hold fast. God has the whole wide world in his hand, and the temptations are there only to remind us there is the godly way, just keep doing right.

Temptation sits in a chair.
Acting innocent as if He does not care.
Watching intently and studying us
mentally. Knowing our every move.
Wanting us to evil approve.
But, know God and His grace,
And your mere existence will
Not be a waste.

# You Are What You Eat

It is good to develop healthy eating habits. Not only is it good to consume foods that will nourish the body but also put you in a better space. It will make your cells function properly. As Bill sat in the doctor's office waiting to be seen he read this in a health magazine. He ponders the thought about what he was going to eat after leaving his appointment. You see Bill was a junk food addict. He had nothing to do with healthy foods. He was overweight with a cholesterol reading of 350, the bad one. When the nurse called Bill back to be seen he gave her his usual look. She would always respond with, "I know what you are thinking Bill, you must die with something." When Bill's doctor called him back it was different this time. The doctor told Bill, "I am worried about your attitude towards this unhealthy lifestyle you've developed over the years. Bill, he says, you don't only eat whatever you desire but you also lead a sedentary life. What are you going to do to extend your life? You just sit at home watching TV and surfing the web. And my God man, Facebook, or should I say fakebook. All that is junk to the mind. You have an unhealthy body and mind. You refuse to eat right or exercise. You should try walking in the fresh morning air, reading some encouraging words from the Good Book. If you are struggling with those habits of yours, seek out a prayer partner, or a lunch buddy who will help you to succeed." Bill had just about enough tongue lashing he was going to stand for. He looked at the doctor and said, "Well the way I see it my big fat unhealthy lifestyle keeps you employed, doesn't it? The doctor shook his head and

*Spiritual Guidance for Common People*

said to Bill, "I'd rather be unemployed if I knew I could win you over with the thought of a healthy body and a saved soul.

We hunger for what is not always good for us or to us, but why? Familiar things keep us on lockdown but try something new. Create new healthy habits physically and spiritually.

# Happiness

Happiness is a state of mind. The word defined is feeling or showing pleasure or contentment. (Merriam-Webster). There are many things that make us happy, money, friends, family, career, and a nice car or house; well, you get the drift. But what is true happiness? You can attain worldly possessions and find out that over time you are not so happy after all and are looking for another piece of happiness.

Back in the seventies there was a song called "Happiness," sung by Charlie Brown and Peanuts. In the song it says, "Happiness is finding a pencil, pizza with sausage, learning to whistle etc. All those things are temporal.

The Word says, "Happiness is to take delight in the Lord and he will give the desires of your heart," (Psalm 37:4). With joy you will draw water from the wells of salvation. (Is. 12:3) "But rejoice inasmuch as you participate in the suffering of Christ, so that you may be overjoyed when his glory is revealed", (Peter 4:13). The words underscored are interchangeable with the word happiness. The Word tells us to seek the Kingdom, and Christ's glory and we will get true happiness. Only then can we receive happiness. When I think about life, I'm reminded that it wasn't the things I've acquired, but what I've done for others. Think about what really gave you happiness in your life, and you'll see God is our true happiness, because He never goes out of style.

# Superwoman

Sandy was known as a Superwoman at her place of work, at church, and community. She was such a worker bee no one could keep up with the energy she had stored up. At work Sandy was an Administrative Assistant. She knew her job very well. She was so proficient her boss did not mind leaving her in charge when he was out of town on business. In church she carried that same energetic spirit. She organized workshops, typed programs, and even kept the pulpit running like a fine running sewing machine. In the community she organized meetings, planned events for the youth. There was nothing she could not do. This is what many people thought of her. Sandy had a secret no one knew about. Her drive and determination were her self-fulling need to be the best regardless and at all costs. Sandy did not realize people began to see her as the one that thinks no one can do it the way she does. Sandy's home life was suffering because of her obligations to work, church, and community. At home she and her husband barely spoke, except when company was over. The stove was always clean because she had no time to cook a meal for her family. Her children were always out of control, and she didn't have a clue. You see it was all about her. Early one Saturday morning, the pastor asked to meet with Sandy. As she drove to the church her mind was in overdrive. She couldn't stop thinking about what project the pastor had for her. She pulled up to the church, the pastor was in his study and the church's saxon was busy tidying up for Sunday morning. Sandy told the saxon, "If I'm out of my meeting with the Pastor

I'll help you get out in time to enjoy the rest of your day." If only she looked back, she would have noticed the saxon slightly shaking his head. "Good morning, Pastor!" Pastor motioned for her to sit. "Sandy." he said, "you have been a real jewel in this church's crown, but I am worried you are not prioritizing what is most important. See Sandy, we are the body of Christ with many members, and each of us has a function, do you understand? If the hand is always doing the walking for the foot the foot can't gain strength and be effective and will lose its ability to walk. The hand will become weak over time and because it is doing the job of the foot. Sandy, we love you, but you are weak in your home life. You have been gifted with many talents, but there is a time and season for you to shine. You don't have to prove to me that you can do it. God is well pleased with your abilities. Now Superwoman go home and be a Super-Wife."

Rejoice in your gifts and talents. This will bring you joy and happiness if the motive is aligned to God's will.

# Challenges

We face challenges each day, at home, at work, and life in general. How we deal with challenges helps us to see how close our prayer life is to God. The relationship we have with God is all we need. Getting intimate with our Father is key. We can go to him with everything. He listens when we don't think he hears us. God is awesome, he is greatly to be praised. How wonderful, I will exalt your name. You were here before the beginning of times and will be here at the end of times. Reflect on how God helped you in challenging times. And Elisha prayed, "Open his eyes Lord, so that he may see." The Lord opened the servants' eyes, and he looked up and saw the hills full of horses and chariots of fire all around Elisha, (2 Kings 6:17). The challenges faced with Elisha's servant were soon dashed by the power of God.

God can do any and everything. We panic when we cannot work through a challenge. We just need to trust the unseen events that are happening all around us every day.

# The Church on the Hill

There once sat a church way up on a hill. No one could miss this church. The drive up the hill was a beautiful iconic, picturesque view. The road was lined with colorful trees. It was a virgin landscape, not touched by construction. In this church was an energetic preacher, moving his church forward. The youth department was second to none, the choirs sang as if they had voices like angels. The Deacons visited the sick and communed with them. The missionary feeds the underprivileged and the undesirables. The Youth cleaned yards, cut grass, and ran errands for the elderly. This church was on fire for the world.

The Pastor of this church had a very large congregation, so he decided to have a revival to really grow the church. He invited a world-renowned evangelist to be the revivalist. This man was basic, he held his services in an old, abandoned factory, and in the summer, services were held outside under a willow tree.

The night of revival the church that sat on the hill had a capacity to hold 5,000 people. But, on the night of the revival the church on the hill was not large enough for the amount that came out for revival. The Revivalist spoke comforting words to the pastor and the crowds. He invited the Pastor and his congregation to his once factory, now a church that housed twice as many as the church on the hill. He explained that the AC no longer worked, but with all the windows open God always sends a nice cool breeze so the cool down would almost require heat.

As the Revivalist opened, he said, "I do things simple, so you can simply live. Life is good but remember to use your resources not simply to be seen, but to simply lead others to Christ who lived a simple life that will bring a greater reward on His return.

# Disguise

Some disguises are so good, you cannot recognize the individual. You believe in what you know to be because their appearance is so convincing. The Devil was in disguise when he convinced Adam and Eve to sin. They believed him to be truthful. The lie was disguised with false truth. He, the Devil, told Eve, "You will certainly not die," the serpent said to the woman. For God knows that when you eat from it your eyes will be opened, and you will be like God, knowing good and evil" (Genesis 3:4). If Eve knew that God made her and Adam his likeness, she would have been able to resist the Devil. How convincing was he. The Devil uses disguises in the home, workplace, school, communities, and even the church. Be vigilant, stay in the spirit and test the Spirit with the Spirit. Dear friends, do not believe every spirit, but test the spirits to see whether they are from God, because many false prophets have gone into the world, (1 John 4:1).

We see more and more everyday people deceived by others who have a deceiving spirit. They will lead you astray because you cannot recognize the deceptive mask that evil wears, wolves in sheep's clothing. Be transparent, no discrepancy in who you represent. De-mask yourself, no disguises please.

# The Businessman

There was once a shrewd businessman. He was so mean, spiteful, and malicious. He gave to charity only to get it back at the end of the year. He gave bonuses only to make his employees work overtime without overtime pay. He gave food to the homeless' food pantry with outdated canned goods.

One day one of his employees asked him if he attended church. His reply was, "I don't see the need, you only waste time listening to someone reading from a book called the Bible. If I were interested in that book, I could read it for myself." The employee came back. "Are you saved?" His response was, "From what, Bible freaks like you." "No, "replied the employee, "from sin, you do know what sin is, don't you?" A little puzzled, he responded, "Why yes, it is a sin to waste time doing nothing and remaining idle." The businessman hoped this would insult the employee and shame her back to work. As she turned to walk away, she stopped and said, "Sir, do you ever sin?" Outraged by this outlandish remark, he burned with anger then said, "Do you see me as a sinner?" She simply smiled and said, "No but God does. This is why he sent his son Jesus to come save you from your sins." "Oh, how does he know if I am sinning?" "I did not tell him; I work to support the poor and lazy, don't I?" "The way I see it, I am helping God by showing a good work ethic, by contributing to the lazy folk that just don't want to work!" "I see she said, I'm a sinner, saved by grace. You cannot buy your way into Heaven or contribute your way in. The only way in is through Jesus Christ himself. He holds the key to the Kingdom of Heaven. So please know your sins will find you out." Irritated at this point the businessman had all he could take of her and asked her to leave. She was no longer employed there. Several weeks later someone came into the office of the businessman. It was one of his managers. He asked the manager if he knew the woman he had fired. The manager responded puzzled by letting him know that no such employee ever worked there He was confused, because he knew she worked for him. The manager picked up on the businessman's' facial expression and said, "Maybe it was your angel."

We need to be careful of what we say or do. We cannot win brownie points with God by what we do outwardly. It is what is in your heart that counts. No pretending, no disguises.

# What's Your Fruit of the Spirit?

In Galatians 5: 22-23, "The Fruits of the Spirits are: love, joy, peace, forbearance, kindness, goodness, faithfulness, gentleness, and self-control." Without these nine attributes we are against what being saved stands for. We live in difficult times. Sure there is nothing new under the sun, but everything seems to be in acceleration. In history there was Alexander Graham Bell with the invention of the telephone. Now there is a cell phone, Internet, eBooks, you name it it's out there. Inventions are being invented at warp speed. We are a competitive nation, and world. We forget to let the fruits reflect who we are. It is good to enjoy the advancement of technology, but remember to always put on those fruits of God Sunday through Saturday. No technology is required to adorn yourself, only love, joy, peace, forbearance, kindness, goodness, faithfulness, gentleness, and self-control.

# Exception or Example

It was the hottest day in the month of July, as we poured cement for our new parking lot in the church's yard. Pastor looked out over the progress and saw his male members that were working diligently and drenched with sweat. "Pastor, one of the church's elderly women pronounced, come get some lemonade." The pastor rolled up his sleeves and walked briskly to the workers and began pushing the wheelbarrow full of soft cement. Immediately the Chair Deacon said, "No Pastor, you are the exception. You don't have to labor." "But the pastor smiled at him and said, "No Deac, I am the example. I must lead by example. The harvest is plentiful, but the laborers are few." (Matthew 9:37-38).

The Pastor was no doubt the leader of his flock, but he chose to be an example. That day the project moved swiftly because they all had a mind to work.

# Watch

To watch is to observe carefully or continuously. When a security guard or patrol is on watch they must be mindful of their surroundings. When we are on watch we, need to be mindful. Christian should always be watchful. The temptation of evil is crouching around every corner, every dark place. If you are not careful you can find yourself engulfed and entangled in a pit. It is so easy to take your eyes off what is right. We need to focus our vision and see the world through a different set of lenses than that of the world.

Just last week I took my eyes off what God had for me. Every dart that was thrown at me hit me, but it did not pierce me. It just gave me a little poke to remind me to stay focused. I focused and began to see the path God wanted me to see.

In the book of Habakkuk 2: 1, "I will stand on my guard post and station myself on the rampart and will keep watch to see what He will speak to me, and how I may reply when I am reproved." Stand guard, and keep watch are key phrases God in Scripture tells and shows us to watch our surroundings and wait to get instructions from Him on how we should govern our lives.

# The Story

Sherry and her friends listened to music in her room when one of her friends said, "What if today is your last day on earth?" What would be the last song you'd like to hear?" Before anyone could answer a loud sound came from outside, and the house shook. Sherry said, "It must be an earthquake. The quake shook and shattered the windows in her house. Her friends began to recite the 23 Psalm; and suddenly Sherry's friends were caught up.

Be ready daily, and watch.

# Convictions

Have you ever been convicted of something you've said or done? If so, that's good. That means you have a conscience. You find yourself mulling over what you've done repeatedly in your head. At times you hear and listen and other times you turn a deaf ear and continue to do what the flesh craves. God is supernatural. He has no lustful desire like the flesh. We need to seek eternal things. The Word should convict you. "Again and again, I sent all my servants, the prophets, to you. They said, "Each of you must turn from your wicked ways and reform your actions. But you have not paid attention or listened to me." Jeremiah 35: 15, 2 Chr. 7: 14.

A dirty vessel cannot pour out fresh water. It needs to be cleaned up first. Be convicted to do right. Aspire to treat people exactly the way God treats you. Help to clean dirty vessels by first cleaning yourself up and when others see the cleanliness of your spirit you will have a testimony to give. The convicted now have convictions in the Word.

# When He Calls

Have you ever heard someone call you, but when you looked you didn't see anyone? Well, God calls us to do great things, but we just look around and don't see what He's saying. "He shall call upon me, and I will answer Him. I will be with Him in trouble-deliver Him and honour him," (Psalm 91:15) "Wherefore the rather, brethren, give diligence to make your calling and election sure: for if ye do these things, ye shall never fall" (2 Peter 1-10).

God calls on all of us to do great things. Great in the human's eyes are not always what God sees as great. Look at the woman who gave. This woman had only one mite to give into offering. While others had far more to place in the temple's treasury. Jesus said, "Truly I tell you; this poor widow has put more into the treasury than all the others. They all gave out their wealth; but she out of her poverty, put everything all she had to live on, (Mark 12:44).

God calls us to give our time, money, and talents; don't disobey or simply ignore the voice of God. We are here for his purpose; we listen to his voice. It is soft and subtle. Don't be so loud, can't you hear him, are you listening?

# The Meat Cutter

It was a hot Summer day. In the city the heat was so extreme that you could not feel the breeze for the buildings that hovered over. On the corner there was a Butcher's Shop, but everyone in the community calls him the meat cutter. He was a stout man with a wide smile, and a slight accent. His laughter was infectious. All the people loved him though they knew very little about him. He would always cut the finest trimmings of meat for single mothers, the elderly, and anyone in need, or who would ask. The meat cutter provided the restaurants. One time the community had a community cookout and ran out of meat and was in need, he gave at no charge. As the summer grew to fall and the leaves glistened as they adorned the trees with yellow, orange, and red. The meat cutter continued to serve the community with delicious fresh meats. The year was coming to an end. Winter approached, everyone was preparing for Christmas and The New Year. Every member of the community received a turkey or roast for the holiday. One day the shop seemed vacant, and a note was left on the door that read, "I thank each of you for all you have done for me. I felt as though you all were my family away from home. I am returning home to take over the family's land. I will herd my father's flock. I am so very grateful for your kindness. I will continue to provide you with all the finest meats.

The meat cutter showed kindness to people who did not really know him, but he knew their needs and provided meat for the body. God is also a provider. He not only provides meat for the body, but for the soul. He is interested in knowing what our needs are and is willing to provide.

# Treasures

Matthew 6:21 puts treasures like this, "For where your treasure is, there your heart will be also." As a child I cherished my toys, especially my stuffed bear Teddy, and not to forget my dolls. Each toy had a name and their own personality. I was particular about who was allowed to play with them. They were cherished treasures. They became my friends, not that that was an oddity because most children develop a friendship with their beloved toys. Oh, how the imagination is impressionable in youth.

When we become adults our treasures change, we desire for things that sometimes are not in the will of God. We should be geared more toward serving others, instead of concentrating on the material treasures that fade away over time, just like my beloved treasured teddy bear and dolls.

In the gospel of (Matthew 6:21), he reminds us in his writings to search our hearts, because whatever is treasured by you is there. So true. I challenge you to store your treasure up in building eternal treasures. I challenge you to show compassion and willingness to serve.

# The Homeless Man

There was a man who had a shopping cart that he carried all his adult life. On day he parked his cart near the edge of the woods. As he entered the convenience store, he looked back at all his worldly possessions. He went inside and began to shop for food and toiletries. As he went to the register to pay for the items, he realized the sock that had his money in it was in his treasured shopping cart. He asked the cashier to hold the items until he had time to retrieve his money. He went to where he left the cart only to see it was gone. Frantically he ran around to see if it rolled off. Unfortunately, it was gone; cart, sock, money, and all he owned. In the store the clerk watches everything that unfold before her eyes and had compassion on the homeless man. The homeless man re-entered the store with sadness on his face. He apologized for not having the money to pay for the items. Unaware the cashier already knew what just transpired. She consoled the homeless man and told him it was going to be alright. She paid for the items and retrieved an old cart the store manager was throwing out. She placed the items in the cart and blessedly watched him out.

God is going to replace our earthly treasures with heavenly treasures on that great getting up morning.

# Powerless to Powerful

Have you ever felt powerless? Being powerless makes a person feel like they are at everyone's will. It is like they have no control over their life. This makes the powerless begin to feel defeated. God has all power. He gives power to the powerless to become like Him. The more you exhibit godly qualities, you gain godly power. You will have the power to love, to forgive, to understand, to have long-suffering, and to have compassion. See, one thing for sure, when you have these power traits there is no room for any powerless notions in your heart. Powerful people don't hate, slander, kill, or kill with words. Powerless people feel strong tearing others down and destroying spirits. But God gave us power to override what the adversary says. "You, O King, are the King of kings, to whom the God of heaven has given the kingdom, the <u>power</u>, and the glory; in your hands he has placed all mankind and beasts of the field and the birds in the sky. Whenever they live, he has made you ruler over them all. You are the head of gold, (Daniel 2: 37-38).

# Missed Calling

Have you ever known someone who's missed their calling? I have. I know a person who was an excellent cook and baker, and for years she said she was going to open a restaurant. If she'd only trusted God and opened her restaurant of *Heavenly Treats, and Tender Meats,* it sure would have been profitable. This was not the actual name but it sure should have been. Her baked goods and delicious meals was so tasty price would have not been an object. Missed calls are in every facet of life. Take for instance, a sportsman never using his talent on the field or court. Never playing the game or teaching the game. God has a calling on each of our lives In the Word it said, "As each one has received a special gift, employ it in serving one another as good stewards of the manifold grace of God. First Peter 4:10, "God has called all of us to spread the Good News that is Jesus Christ our Lord." Don't miss your call to spread the word or your gift and talent.

Today is the day you give others your gift and share your talent generously.

# Too Late!

Cheryl looked through her old scrap book and admired the pictures of herself in her student nursing uniform. She reminisced on the days she sat in her anatomy class. Those were happy days. She just could not help but to think to herself, "what if I just finished, where would I be now?"

It was not Cheryl's fault completely. The program she was in was somewhat skewed. Everyone in the program knew it. Cheryl looked at the photo and recognized her friend Mary who is now a nurse practitioner. It took her 8 years, but she had the drive and determination to purse what God had already ordained. She thought, "What if I had that same drive and determination to push and stay instead of complaining and quit. I'll never know now. I have an aging mother and an ailing spouse. I am bound to being a caregiver to both. I love them both and I know God honors what I am doing. I love what I am doing. But if only I could have advanced my learning, I could do more for them and myself.

God allowed Cheryl to see she could have completed the program by being a dedicated caregiver and a lifelong supporter to the sick. Wait on the Lord and He will strengthen your heart. Yes, he will!

# The Time Has Come

When preparing for events, you must consider all the things you need. Preparation timing is key. You make a list and check it over twice. Once the list is checked off you are now ready for the event you have prepared for. When you have a spiritual list to get you started on your spiritual journey begin the list with, prayer, Bible Study, meditation, and fellowship. In Matthew 25: 1-13, "the five virgins who prepared for the bridegroom's arrival are rewarded, while the five who were not prepared are disowned." In life use the resources that God gives to be successful in all aspects of your life.

# Worship

On one Fall Sunday evening around 6:00 pm, I found myself walking down a long dusty dirt road. The sun was seeping down below the horizon when I spotted a small white wooden church. I was in a bit of melancholy; the mood I was in was depression. Many things were going on in my life at that time. As I approached the small white church, I could hear what sounded like an old upright piano, washboard, and tambourine. I heard praise and singing. I heard shouting, and shout of the highest praise, "hallelujah." I went inside the small white church to see people singing, and shouting just what I heard outside the church. I investigated the faces of the people and tears were rolling down their eyes, hands lifted in praise. I felt drawn in. A warm feeling came over me and I found myself shouting, praising, and even crying except I wasn't sad or depressed. I was rejoicing along with the saints of The Lord for all his goodness. The service was soon ending, I wanted more. Several people hugged one another, some came and hugged me as well. I immediately became sad it was over, but not depressed anymore. Psalms 95:6-7,tells us to come and worship the Lord.

# Heads or Tails

We have heard the saying *Heads or Tails*, or I am the head and not the tail or head over household. On the ship the bow is the head, and the stern is the tail. The rudder controls the direction of the ship. The ship cannot go left or right unless the rudder is pointing in that direction. The Bible tells us in James 3:4, "Or take a ship as an example. Although they are so large and are driven by strong winds they are steered by a very small rudder whenever the pilot wants it to go.

God is the pilot and yes, we can be very small and have much power. We can use our relationship with the Lord Almighty to tap into the power the Holy Ghost has. I have heard it said, "It is not how big is your problem but how big is our God." I like to put it this way, not who is head, but who is controlling that head. David was small in stature when he took on Goliath. But David was the Victor. He allowed God to be head of the ship and guide him to a victory.

# Imposters

Alicia and Matt were the ideal dream couple. They were always together making things happen. If someone was hungry or needed a place to stay, they were your people. Alicia and Matt gave their money and time only when it benefited them. They were competitive to a fault. Their only need was to be on top in everything. The were great over achievers, one uppers, and the first at any event, function or project.

The Life Center was having a rally to raise funds for the new wing. They were to put on the largest rally they have ever done. This would begin with a groundbreaking ceremony. It was to take place in two weeks. A year later, the projected date of the erection of the final stage would complete the project. The rally was to raise as much money as possible so there will be no bill on the wing. The rally went well. They superseded their goal.

Alicia and Matt waited to see who the top contributors were. When the announcement was made their names came in fourth; what a disappointment. The two were flabbergasted by the announcement. Instead of being happy the rally was a success they saw themselves as incompetent. They asked around to see who placed before them. They were surprised when told all other participants were anonymous. There was no shame with Alicia and Matt, they wanted people to know it was them. It was more important to be seen.

**Acts 5:1-11**

Ananias and Sapphira had property and sold it for the cause of kingdom building, but they ended up keeping some of the money. Peter questioned them both separately three hours apart. They were not truthful and paid the ultimate price: death.

What is done in secret is rewarded openly (Matthew 6:3-4).

# What Should We Desire

1 Peter 4:2 states, so as to live for the time in the flesh no longer for human passions but for the will of God. We should desire God's Will. We should desire God's will to live in peace with one another. God created man and woman to live in a cohesive environment, touching and agreeing, cohabiting in harmony. We must live to please the Master even if it does not please us. When we please our desires, we become selfish and not selfless. In a day's time your works should be focused on giving of all you have. Christ did. He gave his life so that we could live an abundant life. What we should share is our time, testimony, and resources. If you want peace know God, and if you want joy, know God. I once saw a church's marquee; No God No Peace, Know God know Peace.

The world is changing daily. You need to desire what God desires for your life. This is a promise without a shadow of doubt peace will be with you all the days of your life.

# A Just God in an Unjust World

God is just even when we don't see justice in this unjust world we live in. Every day we witness all sorts of things: hate, violence, discrimination, racial injustice, and we ask ourselves where is God? God is here. He understands and is actively in charge. When we face injustice, we need to turn and face God. We need to keep our eyes on God. We become lost in the turmoil the world is in. It is not for us to use our justice, it won't work, it never does. Remember what is said in Deuteronomy 31:6, "Be strong and courageous. Do not be afraid or terrified of them, for the Lord your God goes with you; he will never leave you nor forsake you." How comforting are those words. We should feel relief knowing that help is always on the way.

# Don't Use Your Disability to Hinder Your True Ability

One day I was watching the Ellen Show on TV, and on the show an African American male was on the show. He was born with three fingers on one hand and one finger on the other hand. He also had his legs amputated as a small child. He was fitted with prosthesis. He exhibited gratefulness. He said how much he had wanted to play football in school, but the coach told him he couldn't. Instead of looking at the one instance as a rejection he took piano lessons. I listened to the piece that he composed. It was like a Mozart composition, but better because of the lack of all digits on both hands. He had heart and soul in that piece of music, and blessed the ears of the listeners and gave every ear hope to all.

Sometimes we are mentally disabled. We don't move because the world hinders growth. Oh, but how vast is the universe. It is beyond our grasp. God uses those that man would not ordinarily select. What we see as disability God sees the true ability according to 1 Corinthians 1:27, "but God has chosen the foolish things of the world to shame the wise, and God has chosen the weak things of the world to shame the things of which are strong."

# Constructive or Destructive?

According to the dictionary to be constructive is serving to improve. Destructive is to ruin completely, to tear down, demolish. Our tongues can be so destructive at times. We use it to get our point across and call it constructive criticism when it really is a sucker punch or hitting below the belt. If the insults could physically destroy the individual, it would give great elation to the attacker. Constructive criticism when received allows the intended individual insight where improvement can be made. There are times we act on compulsion. We have compulsive actions; we move without thinking. This is where we need guidance. Whether we are the ones receiving the advice or giving it.

What does the Bible say about constructive or destructive words, "Whoever heeds life-giving correction will be at home among the wise. Those who disregard discipline despise themselves, but the one who heeds correction gains understanding; wisdom's instruction is to fear the Lord, and humility comes before honor," Proverbs 15: 31-33. "The tongue also is a fire, a world of evil among the parts of the body. It corrupts the whole body, sets the whole course of one's life on fire, and is itself on fire by hell," James, 3:6.

If you want to know if your words are constructive or destructive follow the Word. The Word never leads us wrong. So, choose your words carefully.

# What Did You Say?

Sandra was a sharp-tongued, middle-aged woman. She was bitter from things in her past. Sandra had a gnarl with her words. She drove people away. She was once engaged to wonderful and understanding man. He saw the good in her, but unfortunately, he was met with an untimely death. This pushed Sandra into a downward spiral. Neighbors, coworkers and church members begin to avoid her. She never had a pleasant word. It was the Sunday the church set aside as fellowship Sunday. On fellowship Sunday it was for the entire church to have a meal in the Fellowship Hall together after service. Sandra came in with the usual unpleasantries. "Who was supposed to keep the burners on?" She grouched as she looked around. No one answered for they knew if they would have, she would ruin the entire meal for everyone. A small scratchy voice from the back of the kitchen area said, "I did." "What did you say?" said Sandra. It was a small wiry older woman that helped wherever needed. Sandra said, "Well in case you did not know, the food could be cold now for not be vigilant." The older woman kindly smiled and said, "I see, you may be right." Sandra was so surprised at the remark. She never received a response like this one. It was always a growl back or a mumble you could not make out. Something inside Sandra felt different. Something she forgot she had in her all the time. Sandra said, "What I mean is the food could be tastier and warm. Thank you for not snapping back at what I said. The old woman said, "It is not a problem. If you did not notice me, I may not have had anyone say anything to me. See honey when you get my age you become invisible to most, no one even recognize that you exist."

Over time the two women became close friends. The words of a bitter middle-aged woman were calmed by an elderly woman looking for someone to say anything to her, just to notice her. We should have a positive response to constructive or destructive criticism.

# The Little Girl's Father

A third-grade class was preparing for *Bring Your Father to school Day.* Chatter was going on in the room about whose father was bigger and better than the others. A little girl spoke up and said, "My father is so big, so rich, that everyone bows down to him." One child bellowed out and said, "My father is a doctor!" The little girl shouted back and said, "My father cures every disease and sickness." Another child said, "My daddy is the CEO!" She blurted back and said, "My Father owns all the cattle on the hill." As the children went on and on, the teacher sat in amazement. She knew the little girl had no father, he passed away when she was a baby. Then the last remark came from the bully in the class, "My dad is a fire fighter, and your dad can't top that." She paused and said, "My father controls the biggest fire, and he is going to burn up all things, just like he did when he flooded the earth." The teacher smiled and said, "Honey your father sure is great isn't he. She said, "Yes ma'am he is more than great. He is awesome!"

Let your life be worth living, your conversation worth giving. Love self, love God, and be well for the best is yet to come. Bless you.

# About the Author

When I first started this book, my mother was battling hypertension. She dealt with this most of her life. It eventually led to hypertensive cardiovascular disease that took her life on November 8, 2019. I, along with my father, were her caregivers for the last three years of her life. I was then drawn closer to the Word. I rested my mind on my mother's wisdom and God's Holy Word. I hope you too will find comfort in the words in this book as you read it and mediate the stories and scriptures that are printed in this book.

I was born in Florence, South Carolina, The second of three children. I was educated all over the world. My father was in the US Army. This broadened my imagination and gave me an insight of people from different walks of life. I always loved writing. I wrote my first story in Hanau, Germany. I was in the third grade. My sister introduced me to pen and paper. I quickly realized I can go anywhere, be anything, and do whatever my imagination would allow just in writing.

I am a wife and mother. I work in the Public School system. I have learned so much from human nature. My experience as a Christian showed me that everyone has a story and in every story is a lesson, and in every lesson, God has the answer.

www.ingramcontent.com/pod-product-compliance
Lightning Source LLC
LaVergne TN
LVHW091321080426
835510LV00007B/590